Using Flannelboards to Teach
Basic Skills

written by Marsha Elyn Wright

illustrated by Patty McCloskey

Grade Pre-K – First Grade

Editors: Stephanie Oberc-Garcia
　　　　　Robert Newman
Art Director: Rita Hudson
Cover Design: Joanne Caroselli
Book Design: Shelly Brown
Graphic Artist: Drew R. Moore

Cover Photography by Color Inc.

J330003 Using Flannelboards to Teach Basic Skills
All rights reserved—Printed in the U.S.A.
Copyright © 2000 Judy/Instructo
A Division of Frank Schaffer Publications, Inc.
23740 Hawthorne Blvd., Torrance, CA 90505

Table of Contents

Tips for Cutouts and Flannelboards

Use flannelboards to teach the alphabet, colors and shapes, numbers, patterning, measurement, classifying, one-to-one correspondence, and other basic skills. When young children interact with a flannelboard, their learning comes alive! These simple ideas will help you create cutouts and flannelboards for the many activities in this book.

Fabric Cutouts

Make cutouts from felt, flannel, or other fabric using your own shapes or the easy-to-trace patterns in the back of this book. Photocopy the pattern pages you want to use, and then cut apart the patterns. Choose the color of fabric for each pattern. Secure the pattern on top of the fabric piece by pinning or taping the pattern to the fabric. Cut around the outer edge of the solid outline to create the shape. Or trace around the pattern using a black felt-tip marker to create a bold outline, and then cut out the shape. There are also manufactured felt cutouts of letters, numbers, basic geometric shapes, and other shapes available at teacher supply stores and craft stores. You can buy fabric that has a holiday- or theme-oriented pattern and make cutouts out of the fabric pictures.

Paper Cutouts

Trace stencils to make cutouts of letters, numbers, and shapes to use with a flannelboard. Use colorful calendar cutouts or cut out illustrations from coloring books and old workbooks! Just glue a piece of felt, sandpaper, or the "hooks" portion of self-sticking Velcro to the back of each cutout. The patterns in the back of this book also create sturdy paper cutouts. Before cutting the patterns apart, laminate the pages, cover them in clear self-stick paper, or photocopy them on different colors of tagboard or thick construction paper.

Storing Cutouts

Store your cutouts inside a resealable plastic bag. Label the bag with the name of the activity and, if appropriate, the page number where it can be found in this book. Place your storage bags in an expandable folder or box. You can also store your cutouts inside a manila folder by stapling both sides of the folder to form a large pocket. Label these folders and file them alphabetically by the title of the activity for a handy reference. You may want to use large envelopes to store your cutouts. This type of storage fits easily in filing cabinets and on shelves.

Making Flannelboards

You can purchase a manufactured flannelboard or try one of these ideas to create your own!

- **Flat Carpet Flannelboard**—Cut out a large rectangle or circle of felt or flannel. When you're doing a flannelboard activity, lay the fabric on your classroom carpet and have the children sit around it.

- **Flat Box Flannelboard**—Open and lay out flat a large cardboard box. Spray adhesive on the front.

  Place a large piece of felt or flannel on the front and smooth out the fabric from the center to the edges. (Attaching a thin layer of foam under the flannel works even better!) Good boxes 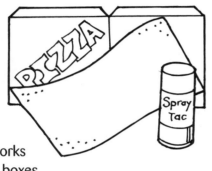 to use are large-size pizza boxes, shipping boxes for large pictures, and packing boxes for posters.

- **Big Box Flannelboard**—Spray adhesive on each side of a large box. Cut out felt or flannel pieces to match the dimensions of the sides of the box. Lay each piece on one side of the box and smooth out the fabric from the center to the edges. As you do an activity, use each side of your flannelboard box to display felt shapes.

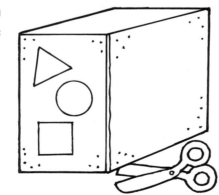

- **Small Flannelboard**—Glue a piece of felt or flannel on a small, lap-sized piece of laminate or sturdy cardboard so it is covered on both sides. These small flannelboards make perfect lap-sized flannelboards for young children.

- **Pressboard or Foamcore Flannelboard**—Buy a large piece (at least 24" x 36") of pressboard or lightweight foamcore, which is available at art supply stores. Cut a length of felt or flannel that is about two inches larger on all sides than the board. Spray the front of the board with a spray adhesive. Lay the fabric on the board leaving a two-inch overlap on all sides. Smooth out the fabric from the center to the edges. Then fold the edges back so that each corner forms a point on the back of the board. Cut off any excess fabric to leave neat corners; then use masking tape or glue to adhere the fabric to the back of the board.

- **Folding Flannelboard**—Collect two large pieces of sturdy cardboard. Cut one piece in half. Use masking tape to attach a smaller piece on each side of the larger piece of cardboard to form two flaps. Spray adhesive on the front of the board. Lay a large piece of felt or flannel over the adhesive and smooth out the fabric from the center to the edges. Use the eraser end of a pencil to press and crease each fold so the flaps still bend. This flannelboard is perfect for displaying on a table when in use and folds up easily for quick storage.

The Alphabet

Manipulating letters on a flannelboard is a visual and tactile way for young children to learn letter names, practice left-right progression, develop fine motor skills, develop visual discrimination skills, and practice sequencing.

Alphabet Hunt

Letter recognition, ABC order

Materials: flannelboard, uppercase and lowercase alphabet cutouts

Before beginning this activity, hide the lowercase cutouts around the classroom. Place the uppercase cutouts in order on the flannelboard, leaving space between each letter.

Point to each letter on the flannelboard as you and the children sing the "ABC Song." Tell the children that they are going on an alphabet hunt to find the lost lowercase letters. Explain that when someone finds a lost letter, he or she puts it next to its matching uppercase letter and then continues to hunt for more letters. After all the letters are found, sing the "ABC Song" once again!

Before and After

ABC order, letter recognition, tactile discrimination

Spread the cutouts on the floor. Place one cutout on the flannelboard. Ask the children this question: *Which letter comes*

Materials: flannelboard, uppercase alphabet cutouts, small paper bags (one for each child)

before this letter? Let the children help you find the letter and place it correctly on the flannelboard. Then ask the children: *Which letter comes **after** this letter?* Let the children again help you find the correct letter. Do this several times to reinforce the concept. Then give each child some cutouts. Ask each question again. This time the child who has the letter that comes *before* shouts, "Before" and the child who has the letter that comes *after* shouts, "After." (If a child has both letters, he or she shouts "before" and "after.") As a challenge, put two or more cutouts in separate small paper bags. Give one bag to each child. Tell the children to keep their bags closed. Place one of the remaining cutouts on the flannelboard. Ask the questions again. Have the children, without looking, touch the letters inside their bags to see if they have the appropriate letters. Those who have the correct letters shout "before" and "after." Keep repeating this activity using different cutouts.

Detective Time

Letter recognition, tactile discrimination

Materials: flannelboard, alphabet cutouts, baseball cap or Sherlock Holmes type of "detective" cap, blindfold

Have the children say the letter name as you place each cutout in sequence on the flannelboard. Choose a child to wear the cap and be the detective. Blindfold the detective and have him or her sit facing the rest of the children. Remove two letters from the flannelboard and give them to the detective. Tell the detective that it is his or her job to name the letters by just touching them. If the detective guesses correctly, let him or her replace the letters on the flannelboard. If the detective is unsure of a letter, offer some clues (for example: *Does the letter have round or straight edges? It is the first letter of ball, balloon, and bug.*) Let the detective choose a new detective for the next round.

Loopy Letters

Fine motor skills, visual discrimination

Materials: flannelboard, uppercase alphabet cutouts, various lengths of pipe cleaners

Tilt the flannelboard. Arrange the cutouts in order on the flannelboard. Using pipe cleaners, form a letter of the alphabet on the flannelboard. Let the children guess the letter. Do this several times. Challenge the children by inviting individuals to form a letter!

Peek-a-Boo Alphabet

Visual discrimination, uppercase and lowercase letters

Materials: flannelboard, 10 large 3" x 3" fabric squares, uppercase and lowercase alphabet cutouts

Prepare for this activity by randomly placing five uppercase letters and their matching lowercase letters in rows on the flannelboard. Cover each letter with a square. Have the children take turns lifting a square, saying the name of the hidden letter, and lifting another square to find the matching lowercase letter. If the letters match, they are left uncovered. If the letters don't match, they are covered again.

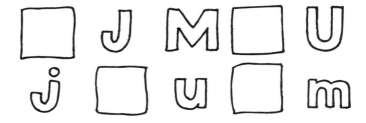

Alphabet Jumble

ABC order, left-right progression

Materials: flannelboard, alphabet cutouts

Choose a sequence of three or four alphabet cutouts and place them in order on the flannelboard. Choose one child to be the "jumbler." Have the rest of the children close their eyes while the jumbler rearranges the cutouts so that they are out of sequence. Then let the jumbler choose someone to place the cutouts in order. Let that child become the next jumbler.

"Chicka Chicka" Flannelboard

Listening, visual-association skills, letter recognition

Materials: flannelboard, lowercase alphabet cutouts, large piece of brown fabric, green fabric, *Chicka Chicka Boom Boom* by Bill Martin Jr. and John Archambault

Position the flannelboard so it's tilted and in a vertical orientation. Make a palm tree by cutting out a brown fabric tree trunk, large green fabric palm leaves, and brown fabric coconuts. Assemble the tree on the board. Give each child two or three letter cutouts to touch and hold while you read aloud *Chicka Chicka Boom Boom* and show the illustrations. Then have the children use their cutouts on the flannelboard to illustrate the story as you slowly reread the book. When the alphabet falls from the tree, let the children rearrange the cutouts into a big pile at the bottom of the tree. As the alphabet climbs out of the pileup, choose children one at a time to rearrange the cutouts. This interactive use of the flannelboard makes learning the alphabet fun!

Alphabet Bugs

Letter recognition, social development, verbal skills

Materials: lap-sized flannelboards (one for each pair of children), *Alpha Bugs* by David A. Carter, uppercase alphabet cutouts (one for each child), scissors, ribbon, fabric scraps, yarn, wiggly eyes, feathers, glue

Read aloud the delightful pop-up alphabet book *Alpha Bugs* by David A. Carter. Talk about each page by asking questions such as these: *How does the bug remind you of the letter? What words on the page begin with the letter?* What other words start with the letter? Then give each child an alphabet cutout. Tell the children to create their own alpha bugs by making facial features and body parts from ribbon, yarn, feathers, and scraps of fabric. Help the children glue wiggly eyes on their bugs. After the children are finished making their bugs, give each pair of children a lap-sized flannelboard. Have the children spend time creating stories with their alphabet bugs on the flannelboards. Invite the partners to share their stories on the classroom flannelboard.

Circle of Letters

Visual discrimination, verbal and thinking skills

Materials: flannelboard, alphabet cutouts, 10-inch-diameter fabric circle

Place the circle on the flannelboard. Place several letter cutouts outside the circle. Ask these questions: *Are any letters alike in some way? How are they alike? Do they have round parts? Do they have straight parts? Do they have both round and straight parts?* As the children answer these questions and find letters that are similar, place the letters on the circle. Review how the letters are alike. Talk with the children about how the remaining letters are different from those on the circle. Repeat this activity using different letters.

Read About the Alphabet

Alpha Bugs, David A. Carter (Simon & Schuster, 1994)

Chicka Chicka Boom Boom, Bill Martin Jr. and John Archambault (Simon & Schuster, 1989)

Colors and Shapes

Help young children learn color names, recognize shapes, practice eye-hand coordination, notice similarities and differences, and develop thinking skills.

Stand-up Colors

Color recognition, color names

Materials: flannelboard, mini-sentence strips, Velcro ("hooks" strip)

Write color names on separate sentence strips. Attach a "hooks" piece of Velcro to the back of each strip. One at a time put a color name on the flannelboard. Have the children say the color word with you. Ask these questions: *What things are this color? Is this color light or dark? Are you wearing this color?* Have the children point to the color on their clothing to reinforce color recognition. Point to one of the color words on the flannelboard and call out its name. Anyone wearing that color has to stand up. The rest of the children stay seated. Point to another color word. Only the children wearing that color stand up. Repeat this activity several times. Watch the delighted faces of the children as they play and learn color names!

Sorting Crayons

Color recognition, color names

Materials: flannelboard, mini-sentence strips, eight crayons in basic colors, self-sticking Velcro

Write the eight crayon color names—*orange, yellow, purple, blue, green, red, brown, black*—on separate mini-sentence strips. Attach a "hooks" piece of Velcro to the back of each crayon and sentence strip. Place each strip along the top of the flannelboard and have the children say the color name with you. Let the children take turns placing a crayon under its color name. Challenge the children. Mix up the crayons and the sentence strips. Let the children take turns matching the crayons and color names on the flannelboard.

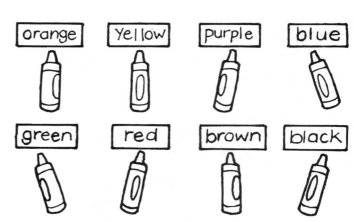

Going Buggy

Color recognition

Materials: flannelboard, several colors of bug cutouts and several leaf cutouts (pattern page 55), wiggly eyes, paint

Decorate the bug shapes. Glue on wiggly eyes, and paint squiggles, dots, and wings on the bodies. Place the bugs on the flannelboard. Tell the children to close their eyes. Choose one child to cover a bug with a leaf. Have the children open their eyes and try to guess which color of bug is covered. The child who guesses correctly covers the next bug. Challenge the children. Cover more than one bug at a time!

Garden Stories

Color recognition, social development, verbal skills

Materials: lap-sized flannelboards (one for each pair of children), bug, flower, and leaf cutouts (pattern page 55)

Group the children by twos. Give each pair of children a lap-sized flannelboard. Let the children use the cutouts to create their own garden stories. Invite partners to share their stories on the classroom flannelboard.

Tiny Seed

Color recognition, verbal skills

Materials: flannelboard, flower cutouts and seed cutout (pattern page 55), pompons

Use pinking shears to cut notch-edged flower shapes. Glue pompons on each flower center. Place the flowers on the flannelboard. Have the children close their eyes while you hide the seed cutout under a flower. Then ask the children: *Which color flower do you think the seed is under?* Let the children agree on a color and recite this verse:

> *Tiny seed, tiny seed,*
> *Playing hide-and-seek.*
> *Lift up the (color) flower,*
> *Let's take a peek!*

Lift up that flower color. If the seed is there, have the children close their eyes and hide it again to repeat the activity. If the seed isn't there, let the children pick another color flower and recite the verse again. Continue the activity until the seed is found! Vary the activity by letting the children take turns hiding the seed.

Shape Match-up

Shape recognition, visual discrimination, fine motor skills

Materials: flannelboard, lap-sized flannelboards (one for each pair of children), several geometric cutouts in repeated colors (pattern pages 52–53)

Arrange three cutouts vertically on the flannelboard so that they are touching. Ask these questions: *Which shapes did I use? Which colors did I use? Which shape is on top? Which shape is in the middle? Which shape is on the bottom?* Group the children by twos. Give each pair of children a lap-sized flannelboard and several geometric cutouts. Rearrange the shapes on your flannelboard. Tell the children to work with their partners and try to copy your picture on their flannelboards. Ask similar questions so that the children can check their work or have the children hold up their work, so you can check it. Repeat this activity several times. Challenge the children by using more than three shapes.

Shape Town

Color and shape recognition, fine motor skills

Materials: flannelboard; several large, middle-sized, and small geometric cutouts in repeated colors (pattern pages 52–53)

Show the children how to arrange cutouts on the flannelboard to form a building, a train, a tree, a house, and other objects. Place the children in small groups, giving each group several cutouts. Tell the children to arrange their cutouts on the floor to make a building, a house, or other object. Invite partners to place their object on the flannelboard. Ask questions that promote color and shape recognition: *Which shapes are used? How many circles are used? How many green shapes are used? Which color is used the most?* After all the objects are displayed, help the children rearrange them into a picture of "Shape Town."

Fuzzy Towers

Shape recognition, fine motor skills

Materials: flannelboard; pipe cleaners; circle, triangle, oval cutouts (pattern pages 52–53)

Tilt the flannelboard. Arrange the shapes to form a tower on one side of the flannelboard. Place the children in groups of three. Give each group three pipe cleaners. Have each group twist and tie the pipe cleaners to form the shapes shown on the flannelboard. Invite each group to "build" a model of the tower by placing their pipe cleaner shapes on the flannelboard.

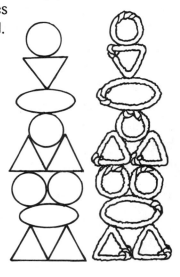

Going on a Shape Hunt

Color and shape recognition, visual discrimination

Materials: flannelboard, six 4" x 4" fabric squares, geometric cutouts (pattern pages 52–53)

Cut out one each of the six geometric shapes from the center of six fabric squares. Place the background pieces on the flannelboard. Spread out the shapes on the floor. Tell the children they are going on a shape hunt in which they will try to match the shapes with their backgrounds on the flannelboard. Let the children take turns naming a shape and placing it on its background. Repeat this activity several times. Then challenge the children by placing the shapes on the flannelboard and having the children match up their backgrounds!

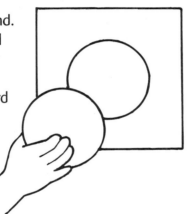

Hidden Pictures

Shape recognition, visual discrimination

Materials: flannelboard, geometric cutouts (pattern pages 52–53), various colors of thick yarn, fabric scraps

Prepare for this activity by practicing simple ways of disguising geometric shapes. For example, turn a red triangle into a slice of pizza by adding pepperoni-shaped pieces of brown fabric and a wavy crust of thick yellow or brown yarn. Disguise a rectangle as a gift by adding a yarn bow. When you are ready for the activity, have the children come to the flannelboard. Tell them you are going to make a hidden picture. Have the children close their eyes while you disguise a shape. Tell the children to open their eyes and look for the hidden shape. Whoever guesses correctly gets to choose the next shape and help you disguise it!

Read About Colors and Shapes

Brown Bear, Brown Bear, What Do You See? Bill Martin Jr. (Henry Holt, 1983)

Color Zoo, Lois Ehlert (Lippincott, 1989)

Mouse Paint, Ellen Stoll Walsh (Harcourt Brace Jovanovich, 1989)

Red Day, Green Day, Edith Kunhardt (Greenwillow, 1992)

Round and Round and Round, Tana Hoban (Greenwillow, 1983)

They Thought They Saw Him, Craig Kee Strete (Greenwillow, 1996)

Numbers

Flannelboard activities are perfect for helping children learn to recognize numbers and number words and practice counting and sequencing.

Counting Warmups

Number recognition, counting, movement, verbal skills

Materials: flannelboard, number cutouts from 1 to 10

Here's a creative way to teach counting while the children exercise! As a morning warmup, have the children stand in front of the flannelboard. As you place the numbers in order on the flannelboard, have the children recite this rhyme and do the movements.

1, 2 . . . Touch my shoe.	(Children touch shoes.)
3, 4 . . . Touch the floor.	(Children touch floor.)
5, 6 . . . Stand like sticks.	(Children stand up straight.)
7, 8 . . . Arms up straight.	(Children lift up arms.)
9, 10 . . . Watch me bend!	(Children bend at waist.)

Rainbow Garden

Counting, color recognition

Materials: flannelboard, several of the same colors of flower-shaped cutouts (pattern page 55), long three-inch-wide strip of green fabric, pompons

Glue pompons on the center of each flower shape. Make a strip of "grass" by cutting slits along one edge of the green strip. Place the grass along the bottom of the flannelboard. Tell the children that you need their help to grow a garden. Spread out the flowers on the floor. Say to the children: *This garden has three yellow flowers and two blue flowers. Who can grow these flowers?* Choose a child to pick out the correct number of yellow and blue flowers and place them on the flannelboard. Repeat by naming new flower colors and choosing children to "plant" them in the garden.

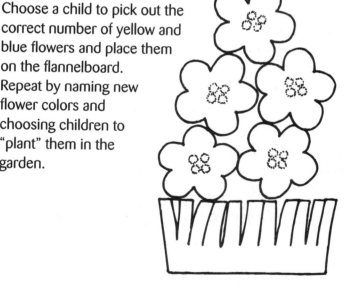

House Numbers

Number words, number recognition

Materials: flannelboard, several copies of number cutouts (1 to 10), several sets of number words *one* through *ten* printed on separate mini-sentence strips, two each of square and triangle cutouts (pattern pages 52–53), Velcro ("hooks" strip)

Attach a "hooks" piece of Velcro to the back of each strip. Use the shape cutouts to make a row of square houses with triangular roofs. Talk with the children about how every house in their neighborhood has a certain set of numbers known as the house's "address." Ask the children to help you put house numbers on the flannelboard homes. Begin by placing a set of number words below one of the houses (for example: *one, five, seven,* and *six*). Read the number words together with your students.

Then choose someone to place the correct number cutouts in order above the house. Do this for each home. As a follow-up, let different children make up new addresses for the class to find!

Calling Out Numbers

Number order, number recognition

Materials: flannelboard, number cutouts (1 to 10 or the number of children you have)

Give each child a number cutout. Call out a number. Have the child holding that number place it on the flannelboard.

Then have the child who holds the number that comes *before* and the child who holds the number that comes *after* place their numbers correctly on the flannelboard.

Watermelon Seeds

Counting, number recognition, number words

Materials: flannelboard, watermelon cutout and 20 black fabric "seeds" (pattern page 56), number cutouts (1 to 20), white fabric paint

Add details to the watermelon. Make a thin green fabric "rind" and glue it to the watermelon. Add a white fabric-paint line on the watermelon next to the green rind.

Put the numbers 1 to 10 in order across the top of the flannelboard and the numbers 11 to 20 across the bottom. Place the watermelon in the middle of the board. Put some seeds on the watermelon. Ask the children: *Which number matches the amount of seeds?* Let a child count the seeds and place the matching number above the watermelon.

How Many Caterpillars?

Number recognition, counting

Materials: flannelboard, different colors of yarn, several leaf-shaped cutouts (pattern page 55)

Cut the yarn into one-inch lengths to make "caterpillars." Tilt the flannelboard. Place the leaves on the flannelboard and put caterpillars on each leaf. Make some leaves have the same amount of caterpillars. Ask questions that require the children to count: *How many leaves have four caterpillars? How many leaves have more than two caterpillars? Which leaf has the most caterpillars?* Depending on the children's abilities, you may want to introduce beginning addition problems by asking questions such as the following: *Which two leaves have a total of five caterpillars? If we add the caterpillars on this leaf and the caterpillar on that leaf, how many are there altogether?*

Jelly Bean Jars

Counting, number recognition, fine motor skills

Materials: flannelboard, number cutouts, five jar cutouts (pattern page 58), small oval-shaped "jelly bean" cutouts in a variety of colors

Place the jelly bean jars on the flannelboard. Place a number above each jar. Ask the children to help you "fill" the jars with jelly beans. Let the children take turns placing the correct amount of jelly beans on each jar. Repeat this activity by letting the children take turns placing different numbers above the jars and filling them.

What's My Number?

Number recognition, number sense

Materials: flannelboard, rectangle cutout (pattern page 52), number cutouts (1–10)

Put the rectangle on the flannelboard. Have the children close their eyes while you hide a number under it. Tell the children to open their eyes and try to guess which number is hidden. Before each guess, give the children a clue: *This number is more than ____. This number is less than ____.* Choose a child to be the "checker." Each time the children make a guess, have the checker peek under the rectangle to see if the guess is correct. (The checker shouldn't let the other children see the number.) After a correct guess, let the checker choose a new checker.

Over in the Meadow

Counting, listening skills, visual-association skills

Materials: flannelboard; small circle cutouts—23 brown, 7 yellow, 16 green, 9 pink (pattern page 53); number cutouts 1–10; *Over in the Meadow* by Louise Voce

Arrange the numbers vertically on the left side of the flannelboard. Spread out the circles on the floor. As you read aloud the rhyming story, choose children to place the appropriate number and color of circles by each number. (The colors correspond to the colors of the animals in the rhyme.) Check the flannelboard by matching it with the illustrations on the last pages!

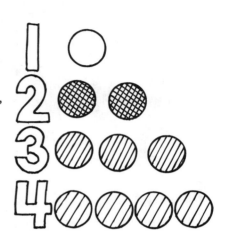

Counting Mice

Counting, listening skills, visual-association skills, fine motor skills

Materials: flannelboard; 10 mouse cutouts, 1 snake cutout, and 1 jar cutout (pattern page 58); fabric paint; wiggly eye; yarn; *Mouse Count* by Ellen Stoll Walsh

Use different colors of felt for the mice bodies and ears. Glue ears of one color on a body of a different color. Squeeze dabs of fabric paint for eyes and glue on yarn tails. For the snake, glue on a wiggly eye and make fabric-paint stripes on the body.

Place the cutouts on the flannelboard. Read the story, moving the cutouts when appropriate. Then give one child the snake, one child the jar, and two children the mice. As you slowly reread the story, let the children move the cutouts on the flannelboard. Put the children without cutouts in two groups—one group makes squeaks for the mice; the other group makes hissing noises for the snake. As you read, signal each group to make its sound effects. When the mice "uncount" themselves in the story, let the children count backwards too! The children will enjoy this story so much they'll ask you to tell it again!

Read About Numbers

Mouse Count, Ellen Stoll Walsh (Harcourt Brace Jovanovich, 1991)

One Gorilla, Atsuko Morozumi (Farrar, 1990)

Over in the Meadow, Louise Voce (Candlewick Press, 1994)

Ten Black Dots, Donald Crews (Greenwillow, 1986)

Up to Ten and Down Again, Lisa Campbell Ernst (Lothrop, Lee & Shepard, 1986)

Ordering

Flannelboard activities are great to help teach young children about ordinal numbers, chronological order, and comparisons.

The Bugs Go Marching

Ordinal numbers, word recognition, verbal skills

Materials: flannelboard, seven bug cutouts in different colors (pattern page 55), mini-sentence strips, Velcro ("hooks" strip) pipe cleaners or yarn for legs

Write *first, second, third, fourth, fifth, sixth,* and *seventh* on separate sentence strips. Attach a "hooks" piece of self-sticking Velcro to the back of each strip. Place the strips in order on the flannelboard. Spread the bug cutouts on the floor. Have the children choose an ordinal number and a color, and then recite this chant:

> Tiny bugs go marching,
> All in a row.
> (ordinal number) comes the (color) bug,
> Hi dee, hi dee, ho!

Choose a child to correctly arrange the bugs on the flannelboard after the chant. Continue this activity until all the bugs are in order.

Copycats

Ordinal numbers, shape and color recognition

Materials: flannelboard, pairs of six geometric cutouts in different colors (pattern pages 52–53), long three-inch-wide strip of fabric

Arrange one set of cutouts in a row on the flannelboard and cover them with the strip. Spread out the other set on the floor. Tell the children: *I want you to be copycats and copy the order of the cutouts hidden under the felt. I will give you clues.* Then say clues using ordinal numbers such as the following: *The green triangle is third.* Let children take turns placing the cutouts in order on the flannelboard. When the children finish, lift up the fabric to see if the two rows match! Repeat the activity again and again using different ordering.

Speedway
Ordinal numbers, word recognition

Materials: flannelboard, 7 car cutouts in different colors and 14 black wheel cutouts (pattern page 57), long strip of two-inch-wide white fabric, mini-sentence strips, brass fasteners, and Velcro ("hooks" strip)

Attach black felt "wheels" on each racecar with a brass fastener. Write *first, second, third, fourth, fifth, sixth,* and *seventh* on separate mini-sentence strips. Attach a "hooks" piece of self-sticking Velcro to the back of each strip. Place the strip of white "speedway" on the flannelboard and put the racecars on it. Spread the ordinal strips on the floor. Let the children take turns placing the correct ordinal above the car. Ask the children this: *The (color) car is in which place in the race?* Let the children match up the ordinals and cars in different sequences again. Then challenge them! Spread the cars and ordinals on the floor. Have the children take turns picking a car and its position and choosing someone to place the car and ordinal on the speedway.

Hungry Mice
Ordinal numbers, counting

Materials: flannelboard, 10 mouse cutouts (pattern page 58), one small fabric triangle

Cut holes in the triangle and round the corners to make it look like a piece of cheese. Place the mice in a row on the flannelboard. Have the children close their eyes while you hide the cheese under one of the mice. Tell the children to guess which mouse has the cheese. Let the children take turns telling you the following: *Lift up the (ordinal number) mouse.* Continue until the cheese is found. Whoever guesses correctly gets to hide the cheese the next time!

"Cupcake" Party

Ordinal numbers, counting, fine motor skills

Materials: flannelboard, 10 cupcake cutouts and 20 candle cutouts (pattern page 54)

Invite the children to your "cupcake" party! Line up the cupcakes on the flannelboard. Place the candles along the bottom of the board. Tell the children you need their help putting candles on the cupcakes. Let the children take turns placing candles on the cupcakes. Give the children directions such as the following: *Please put three candles on the second cupcake.* After all the candles are in place, sing together "Here's a cupcake for you!" to the tune of "Happy Birthday to You!"

Pet Store

Ordering, word recognition

Materials: flannelboard; one each of the fish, mouse, rabbit, frog, bird, cat, and dog cutouts (pattern pages 58, 62–63); mini-sentence strips; wiggly eyes; Velcro ("hooks" strip)

Add details to the animal cutouts. Glue on wiggly eyes. Trim the bird's tail with pinking shears and glue on another wing. Use fabric paint to make noses, eyes, and whiskers. Glue on yarn tails. Layer different sizes of varying colors of circles to make the frog's eyes. Glue on a pompon for the rabbit's tail.

Write *first, next,* and *last* on separate sentence strips. Attach a "hooks" piece of self-sticking Velcro to the back of each strip. Arrange the strips vertically on one side of the flannelboard. Place the cutouts randomly on the other side. Announce that each child will get a turn "buying" three pets at the pet store. Each time the shopper buys a pet, have him or her place the pet next to the appropriate sentence strip. Then have the children say this chant three times filling in the appropriate words:

(child's name), (child's name),
Shopped at the store.
*The (animal's name) was the (**first, next,** or **last**) pet,*
Did (child's name) buy one more? (Children shout YES two times and NO the last time.)

Alphabet Races

Ordering, letter recognition

Materials: flannelboard, lowercase alphabet cutouts, *Chicka Chicka Boom Boom* by Bill Martin Jr. and John Archambault

Read aloud *Chicka Chicka Boom Boom,* pointing out the words *next, then,* and *last* in the text. Place the children in small groups. Let each group "race" to alphabetize a set of letters on the flannelboard. To start each race, tell the children to shout *boom, boom!* Then drop a set of sequential letters on the floor. Have the group that's racing try to order the letters on the flannelboard before the rest of the children finish chanting the "Skit scat" rhyme from the book. These races are such fun that the children will want to do them over and over! (You might want to create a coconut tree on the flannelboard. See description on page 8.)

Twelve Tiny Hungry Ants

Ordering, grouping, skip counting

Materials: flannelboard, 12 red oval cutouts for "ants," checkered-fabric square cutout, muslin or other fabric cut in shape of an "ant hill," *One Hundred Hungry Ants* by Elinor J. Pinczes

Place the ant hill on one side of the flannelboard. Put the ants on the ant hill. Place the fabric square "picnic blanket" on the other side of the flannelboard. Read aloud *One Hundred Hungry Ants.* Afterwards, tell the children you have 12 hungry ants that want to get from the ant hill to the picnic blanket. Have the children help you find different groupings for the ants as they travel from the hill to the blanket. First, order the ants in one long row. Next, group the ants by twos in a line. Help the children count the ants by twos. Then group the ants by threes, fours, and sixes. Count the ants each time so the children understand there are always 12 ants. Let different children help you arrange the ants into the groups. Each time you regroup the ants, move them closer to the picnic blanket. Try this activity again using six ants.

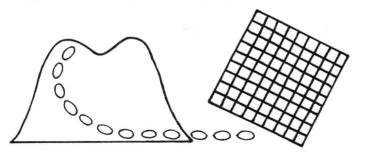

Read About Ordering

Chicka Chicka Boom Boom, Bill Martin Jr. and John Archambault (Simon & Schuster, 1989)

One Hundred Hungry Ants, Elinor J. Pinczes (Scholastic, 1993)

Amounts and Sizes

These flannelboard activities will give young children practice in recognizing more and fewer, making comparisons, and noticing size differences.

Eggs and Leaves
More and fewer

Materials: flannelboard, two large leaf-shaped cutouts, mini-sentence strips, white pompons, Velcro ("hooks" strip)

Write *fewer* and *more* on separate sentence strips. Attach a "hooks" piece of self-sticking Velcro to the back of each strip. Place the leaves and the sentence strips on the flannelboard. Put a different number of pompon "eggs" on each leaf. Say to the children: *There are caterpillar eggs on each leaf. Which leaf has more eggs? Which leaf has fewer eggs?* Ask a child to count the eggs on each leaf and move the labels *more* and *fewer* over the appropriate leaves. Repeat this activity several times. Then let the children place the eggs on the leaves.

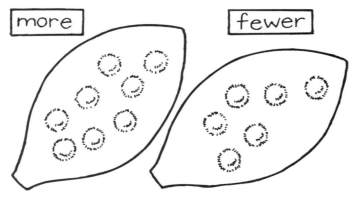

Flowers in a Jar
More and fewer

Materials: flannelboard, several flower cutouts (pattern page 55), two jar cutouts (pattern page 58), several thin strips of green fabric for the flower stems, mini-sentence strips, Velcro ("hooks" strip)

Write *fewer* and *more* on separate mini-sentence strips. Attach a "hooks" piece of self-sticking Velcro to the back of each strip. Put the jars on the flannelboard. Place *more* under one jar and *fewer* under the other. Spread out the flower and stem cutouts on the floor. Let the children take turns matching a stem and a flower and placing them in each jar so one jar has *more* flowers and the other jar has *fewer* flowers. Have the rest of the children count the flowers. Switch the labels after several children have had a turn and continue the activity.

Comparing Watermelons

Fewest, more, and most

Materials: flannelboard, three watermelon cutouts and 20 small black fabric "seeds" (pattern page 56; see description of how to decorate watermelon on page 15), mini-sentence strips, Velcro ("hooks" strip)

Write *fewest, more,* and *most* on separate sentence strips. Attach a "hooks" piece of self-sticking Velcro to the back of each strip. Place the watermelon cutouts on the flannelboard. Place a different amount of oval "seeds" on each watermelon. Choose two children to count the seeds. Ask the children the following: *Which watermelon has the fewest seeds? Which watermelons have more seeds? Which watermelon has the most seeds?* Place *fewest, more,* and *most* over the appropriate watermelons. Repeat this a few times. Invite the children to take turns placing seeds on the watermelons.

Each time ask the children these questions: *Which watermelon has the fewest seeds? Which watermelons have more seeds? Which watermelon has the most seeds?* As a follow-up, cut up real watermelon for a juicy treat!

Cats on a Fence

Big, bigger, biggest

Materials: flannelboard, two long strips of brown fabric, two short strips of brown fabric, mini-sentence strips, six cat cutouts in varying sizes (pattern page 63), Velcro ("hooks" strip)

Arrange the strips of brown along the bottom of the flannelboard to create a "fence." Write the words *big, bigger,* and *biggest* on separate mini-sentence strips. Attach a "hooks" piece of self-sticking Velcro to the back of each strip. Place three cat cutouts on the flannelboard. Have a child place the cats along the fence in order from big to biggest. Place the labels over the appropriate cats. Repeat this a few times. Let children take turns choosing any three cats and arranging them along the fence. Have the rest of the children guess the order of the cats. (The cats might end up being arranged in an unusual sequence such as *biggest, big, bigger.*)

The Animal World

Small, smaller, smallest

Materials: flannelboard, mini-sentence strips, several animal cutouts in varying sizes (pattern pages 62–63), Velcro ("hooks" strip)

Write the words *small, smaller,* and *smallest* on separate mini-sentence strips. Attach a "hooks" piece of self-sticking Velcro to the back of each strip. Place the strips in a row at the top of the flannelboard. Place three animal cutouts of varying sizes on the floor. Have the children help you arrange the animals from small to smallest on the flannelboard under the appropriate labels. Then choose three new animal cutouts in varying sizes. Ask the children the following: *Which animal is small? Which animals are smaller? Which animal is the smallest?* Choose a child to place the animals under the appropriate labels on the flannelboard. Repeat this a few times. Invite the children to choose three animals and order them on the flannelboard.

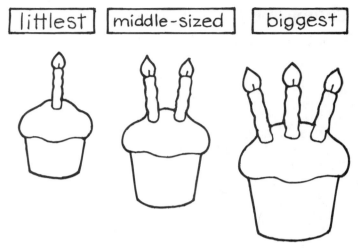

Candles and Cupcakes

Biggest, middle-sized, littlest; counting

Materials: flannelboard, six cupcake cutouts in varying sizes and 20 candle cutouts (pattern page 54), fabric paint

Add details to the cupcakes with dots of fabric paint.

Place three of the cupcakes on the flannelboard. Ask the children: *Which is the littlest cupcake? Which is the middle-sized cupcake? Which is the biggest cupcake?* Let the children help you line up the cupcakes by size (littlest to biggest or biggest to littlest). Instruct the children to do something like the following: *Put two candles on the littlest cupcake.* Invite someone to do this. Give another direction such as the following: *Put five candles on the middle-sized cupcake.* After each instruction, invite someone to put the appropriate number of candles on the cupcake. Rearrange the cupcakes and repeat the activity.

Gone Fishing

Noticing size differences, word recognition, visual memory

Materials: flannelboard, long 4-inch-wide strip of light blue fabric, four fish cutouts in varying sizes (pattern page 62), *Blue Sea* by Robert Kalan, Velcro ("hooks" strip)

Place the strip of blue along the bottom of the flannelboard to create "water." Write *little, big, bigger,* and *biggest* on separate sentence strips.

Attach a "hooks" piece of self-sticking Velcro to the back of each strip. Read aloud *Blue Sea* and talk about the size of each fish in relation to the size of the other fish in the story. Place the fish cutouts on the flannelboard. Have the children take turns placing the fish in the "water" in order from littlest to biggest and from biggest to littlest. After a child arranges the fish, place each label above the appropriate fish. Challenge the children! Have them close their eyes; then take away one of the fish. When they open their eyes, say to the children, *I've gone fishing. Which size fish did I catch?* Whoever guesses correctly goes fishing the next time!

Creeping Caterpillars

Long, longer, longest

Materials: flannelboard, six caterpillar cutouts in varying sizes (pattern page 60), mini-sentence strips, fabric paint, Velcro ("hooks" strip)

Add facial features and body stripes on each caterpillar with fabric paint.

Write the words *long, longer,* and *longest* on separate mini-sentence strips. Attach a "hooks" piece of Velcro to the back of each strip. Randomly place three caterpillars of varying sizes on the flannelboard. Have the children help you arrange the caterpillars from long to longest. Place the labels above the appropriate caterpillars. Have the children close their eyes while you mix up the caterpillars. Invite children to rearrange them under the appropriate labels. Have the children take turns picking out caterpillars and arranging them in order.

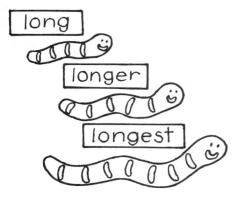

long
longer
longest

Read About Amounts and Sizes

Blue Sea, Robert Kalan (Greenwillow, 1979)

Biggest, Strongest, Fastest, Steve Jenkins (Scholastic, 1995)

Patterning

Flannelboard activities are perfect for helping children learn to recognize numbers and number words and practice counting and sequencing.

Missing Pieces

Identifying and creating a pattern, visual memory

Materials: flannelboard, three of each geometric cutout (pattern pages 52–53)

Create a simple pattern on the flannelboard using the cutouts. (For example, *triangle-circle-circle-square*) Ask the children: *What comes next?* Then have the children close their eyes while you take away one piece of the pattern. Have the children open their eyes and guess the missing piece. Repeat this a few times; then take away more than one piece at a time to challenge the children!

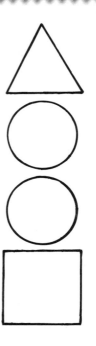

What Comes Next?

Identifying and creating a pattern

Materials: flannelboard, six of each geometric cutout (pattern pages 52–53; make same shapes one color)

On the flannelboard use the cutouts to make a simple *AB* pattern such as *square-circle-square-circle*. Ask the children, *What comes next?* Let the children take turns placing the next cutout in the pattern. Create a more difficult pattern, such as *circle-circle-square-triangle*. Ask different children to place the next cutout in the pattern. Invite a child to create a pattern on the flannelboard. Choose other individuals to continue the pattern.

Building Skyscrapers

Identifying a pattern, fine motor skills

Materials: flannelboard, several of each geometric cutout (pattern pages 52–53; make same shapes one color)

Use a pattern (such as *square-square-circle-rectangle*) with the cutouts on the flannelboard to create a skyscraper. Ask the children to tell you what comes next. Have a child build a skyscraper on the flannelboard following the same pattern. Build a new skyscraper using a different pattern. Invite the children to build skyscrapers following the new pattern.

J330003 Using Flannelboards to Teach Basic Skills

Reach the Cheese!

Identifying and creating a pattern

Materials: flannelboard, 12 mouse cutouts using three different colors for the bodies (pattern page 58; see description of how to decorate mice on page 17), yellow square cutout (pattern page 52)

Cut holes in the square to create a "slice of Swiss cheese." Place the cheese on the right side of the flannelboard. Tell the children that the mice are hungry and are trying to get to the cheese. Create a simple pattern with the mice on the flannelboard (for example: *gray-white-white-brown).* Begin the pattern to the left of the cheese and work toward the cheese. Ask different children to place what comes next in the pattern until the mice meet the cheese. Invite different children to start a pattern of mice. Choose other children to take turns continuing the pattern so that the mice reach the cheese!

"Beaded" Necklaces

Identifying and creating a pattern

Materials: flannelboard, small oval cutouts in a variety of colors (10 of each color), two 12-inch strips of fabric

Place the strips horizontally on the flannelboard. Place ovals in a simple pattern on one strip to create a "beaded necklace" (for example, *red-yellow-blue).* Ask the children, *What comes next?* Let the children take turns finishing the pattern. Take off the ovals and create a new pattern on one strip. Have different children take turns creating the same pattern on the other strip. As a follow-up, cut out geometric shapes from paper and punch a hole in the center of each shape. Let each child slide the shapes in a simple pattern onto a length of yarn to make a necklace to wear home!

Read About Patterned Language

The Grouchy Ladybug, Eric Carle (HarperCollins, 1977)

The Napping House, Audrey Wood (Harcourt Brace Jovanovich, 1984)

Ten in a Bed, Mary Rees (Little Brown, 1988)

Graphing

Flannelboard activities will help introduce young children to the fun of making and reading graphs.

Our Class

Making and using a picture graph

Materials: flannelboard, boy and girl cutouts (pattern page 59; make enough of each to represent every child in your classroom), tiny yellow fabric squares, tiny brown fabric squares, tiny black fabric squares

Give each child either a boy or girl cutout. Ask the children: *How many girls are in our class? How many boys are in our class?* Record the answers by helping the children make a picture graph with their cutouts on the flannelboard. Then ask them, *Are there more boys than girls in our class?* Next, place three boy cutouts and three girl cutouts vertically on the flannelboard. Place a different color square on each boy and on each girl to represent hair colors. Make a pile of the other squares. Have the children look at one another to answer these questions: *How many boys have blond hair? How many boys have brown hair? How many boys have black hair?* (Then ask these questions about the girls.) Record the answers by placing the appropriate number of yellow, brown, or black square cutouts next to the corresponding boy and girl. Then ask these kinds of questions: *What color hair do most boys have? Do more girls have black hair than brown hair?*

We All Scream for Ice Cream

Making and using a picture graph

Materials: flannelboard; several each of small pink, white, and brown circle cutouts (pattern page 53); three long brown fabric triangles

Place the triangles in a row on the flannelboard. Place one color circle on top of each triangle. Spread out the rest of the circles on the floor. Say to the children: *Here are three "ice cream cones." Which flavor of ice cream do YOU like best?* Record the children's answers by having each child take a color circle that matches his or her favorite flavor of ice cream and place it above the appropriate cone. Discuss the graph information. Ask these kinds of questions: *Which flavor is the most favorite? Which flavor is the least favorite? Do more children like _____ than _____?*

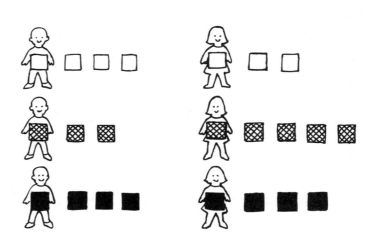

How Many?

Making and using bar graphs

Materials: flannelboard; several small, narrow rectangles (one for each child); number cutouts

Give each child a rectangle. Place *0, 1, 2, 3, 4,* and *5* in a column on the left side of the flannelboard. Ask the children a question such as the following: *How many pets do you have?* One at a time let each child place his or her rectangle next to the appropriate number, forming a bar with the other rectangles in that row. After the graph is finished, ask the children questions such as these: *How many children have one pet? How many children have five pets? How many pets do most children have?* Then lift off the rectangles, give one to each child, and ask another question. Let the children respond the same way to create a new bar graph! Repeat this routine several times.

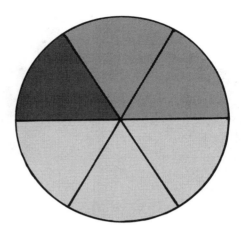

Pizza Time

Reading a circle graph

Materials: flannelboard, three different colors of large circle cutouts cut into sixths, mini-sentence strips (one for each child), Velcro ("hooks" strip)

Use different colors of six wedges to form one circle graph on the flannelboard. Place wedges that are the same next to one another. Write each child's name on a sentence strip. Attach a "hooks" piece of Velcro to the back of each strip. Choose three children's names and place them on the flannelboard. Beside each name place a different color wedge to make a key for the graph. Say to the children: *For lunch, I made a pizza and cut it into six slices to share with (names of the three children). This circle graph shows how many slices of pizza each child ate.* Then ask the children: *How many slices of pizza were there altogether? Who ate the most slices of pizza? Who ate the fewest slices? Did everyone eat the same number of slices?* Change the circle graph and use different children's names to represent each color of wedge. Ask the same kinds of questions.

Measurement

These activities will give the children practice in estimating and measuring length and height using standard and nonstandard units of measure.

Measuring With Real Feet
Nonstandard unit of measure, length

Materials: flannelboard, 20 foot-shaped cutouts, a child's jump rope

Place the children into three groups. Lay the jump rope straight on the floor. Take off your shoes. Tell the children you are going to measure the length of the jump rope with your feet. Starting at one end of the jump rope, walk *heel-toe-heel-toe* the length of the rope. Have the children count the number of feet it takes. Place that many foot cutouts in a row on the flannelboard. Repeat this activity by asking a child to measure the length again using his or her feet. Record the length on the flannelboard. Talk about the differences between the two lengths (the foot sizes are different). Try this activity again by measuring the length of other items in the classroom—a broom, a pointer, and a rug.

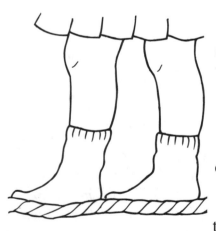

Which Is the Tallest?
Standard unit of measure, height

Materials: flannelboard, 10 one-inch-long fabric rectangles, animal cutouts with varying heights (pattern page 63), number cutouts

Place the animal cutouts on the flannelboard. Use the rectangles to measure the height of one of the animals. Have the children count the inches with you. Place the corresponding number cutout above the animal. Ask the children, *Which of the other animals is closest in height to this animal?* Invite many responses. Measure each animal's height and have the children count with you to find out the answer.

Wrapping Gifts
Standard unit of measure, height, width

Materials: flannelboard, four fabric squares in varying sizes and colors, four cutouts that match the heights and widths of the fabric squares (see the variety of patterns at the back of this book; use patterns that could be toys), 12-inch length of yarn

Use a black permanent marker to make inch marks on the yarn. Place the four "toy" cutouts and the square "gift boxes" on the flannelboard. Tell the children that you need help to find the right size box for each toy.

Start with the smallest toy. Use the yarn to measure its length and width. Have the children count the inches with you. Then measure different boxes to see which box is right for the smallest toy. Place the toy on top of the correct box. Do this for each toy.

Inching Along
Standard unit of measure, estimating, length

Materials: flannelboard, variety of long animal cutouts in varying numbers of inches (pattern pages 55, 58, 60, 62–63), 12 one-inch-long fabric rectangles, *Inch by Inch* by Leo Lionni

Read aloud *Inch by Inch.* Talk with the children about how the inchworm measured different animal characters. Then place three animals of different lengths in a row on the flannelboard. Place the inch cutouts side by side to measure the length of the first animal. Have the children count the inches with you. Say to the children: *If the (name of animal) is (number) inches long, how long do you think the (name of the next animal) is?* Invite the children to make guesses. Measure the animal using the inch cutouts. Have the children count the inches with you again. Repeat this routine with the third animal. Place three new animals in a row on the flannelboard. Do the activity again. This time let the children take turns measuring the length of the animals.

Read About Measurement

Inch by Inch, Leo Lionni (Astor-Honor, 1962)

How Big Is a Foot? Rolf Myller (Atheneum, 1962)

Sequencing

These flannelboard activities will give the children practice in sequencing numbers, actions, and story events.

Number Mix-up

Sequencing numbers

Materials: flannelboard, number cutouts

Sequence a set of numbers on the flannelboard. Point to each number and have the children say its name with you. Tell the children to close their eyes while you mix up some of the numbers. Ask for a volunteer to put the numbers in correct sequence. If the child needs help, invite the whole class to help sequence the numbers. Let the child who volunteers mix up the next set of numbers.

Look Out!

Sequencing actions

Materials: flannelboard, six different animal cutouts (pattern pages 55, 58, 60, 62–63), *Look Out, Bird!* by Marilyn Janovitz

Read aloud *Look Out, Bird!* and talk with the children about how one animal's action caused another action. Then place the six cutouts on the flannelboard. Let the children help you make up a story about animal actions while you sequence the cutouts. The children will enjoy this imaginative play so much they'll want to create another story using a different sequence of actions!

Number Skip

Sequencing numbers, skip counting

Materials: flannelboard; *2, 4, 6, 8,* and *10* number cutouts

Sequence the numbers by twos on the flannelboard. Point to each number and have the children say its name with you. Show the children how each number moves up by two. Tell the children to close their eyes while you mix up a couple of numbers. Choose someone to sequence the numbers correctly. Let that child mix up the numbers for another round of play.

Catching Fish

Sequencing numbers, number recognition

Materials: flannelboard, number cutouts, six fish cutouts (pattern page 62), four-inch-wide strip of blue fabric, six paper clips, wooden dowel, magnet, string

Make a fishing pole by tying one end of a string to a dowel and the other end to a magnet. Place the blue fabric along the bottom of the flannelboard to make a "pond."

Attach a paper clip to each fish. Place the fish cutouts in the pond.

Choose a set of six numbers in sequence and randomly place one number above each fish. Have the children take turns "catching the fish" in sequential order by touching the magnet to the paper clip.

Packing for a Picnic

Sequencing objects, listening

Materials: flannelboard, food cutouts (pattern pages 60–61), large basket-shaped fabric cutout

Tell the children you need their help to pack food for a picnic. Place the picnic basket on the flannelboard. Spread out the food cutouts on the floor. Tell the children the sequence in which you want to pack the food—for example: *pear, apple, strawberry, plum.* Let the children take turns sequencing the objects as you tell them new sequences.

Tell a Story

Sequencing animal characters, listening

Materials: flannelboard, four animal cutouts (pattern pages 58, 60, 62–63), other cutouts as needed for the storytelling (optional)

Place the animal cutouts randomly on the flannelboard. Choose someone to help you sequence the animals in the order they appear in the story you will tell. Then make up a simple story using the animal characters in a certain sequence such as the following:

One hot day, Dog jumped in the pond. Snake slithered by and said, "Hi, Dog! May I swim too?"

"Sure!" said Dog. So Snake slid into the pond.

Along came Cat. "Hi, Dog! Hi, Snake!" called Cat. "What a fine day for the pond!" She twitched her tail and sat because cats don't swim.

Hi, Cat!" called Dog and Snake.

Suddenly there was a big SPLASH! "What was that?" shouted the animals. They all ran from the pond and hid!

"Hey!"gurgled a voice from under the water. "Where is everybody?" Dog, Snake, and Cat peeked out from where they were hiding. They all laughed. It wasn't scary after all. It was only Frog splashing about in the pond!

Tell a new story. Choose different children to help sequence the animals.

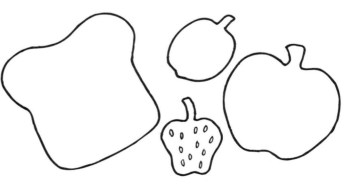

Let's Make a Sandwich

Sequencing food, listening

Materials: flannelboard, two brown bread cutouts (pattern page 54), one green pickle cutout (pattern page 61), one green lettuce-leaf-shaped cutout, one yellow square (pattern page 52), two circle cutouts (one brown and one red; pattern page 53)

Cut holes in the square so that it resembles Swiss cheese. Use pinking shears to cut a notched-edged pickle. Use the brown circle for a sausage slice and the red circle for a tomato slice.

Tell the children that you need their help to make a sandwich. Give out each cutout to a child. Say to all the children: *Let's build a sandwich! First take a slice of bread. Next put a lettuce leaf on the bread. Then put . . .* (continue this pattern until all the cutouts are sequenced). As you are talking, let the children holding the appropriate cutouts place them in order on the flannelboard.

Try this again using different children and a new sequence.

Rainbow Rectangles

Sequencing colors, listening, oral language

Materials: flannelboard, six rectangle cutouts (one each of purple, blue, green, yellow, orange, red; pattern page 52)

Teach the children the "Rainbow Colors" song (sung to the tune of "Twinkle, Twinkle Little Star"):

Rain and sunshine,
In the sky,
Make a rainbow,
Way up high,
Colors purple, blue, and green,
Yellow, orange, and red are seen.
Rainbow smiling way up high,
When I look up in the sky!

Randomly place the colors of rectangles on the flannelboard. While the children sing the song, let individuals take turns placing the colors in sequence on the flannelboard.

Not Last Night But the Night Before . . .

Sequencing objects, listening, oral language

Materials: flannelboard, six cutouts

Spread the cutouts on the floor. Teach the children this rhyme:

Not last night but the night before,
Three funny things came knockin' at my door.
"Knock, knock, knock"
Went the ____ and the ____ and the ____!

Choose a child to arrange the cutouts on the flannelboard in the sequence of "what came knocking." Let that child pick the next person to arrange a new sequence of cutouts. Challenge the children by having them sequence four or five things!

A Hungry Caterpillar

Sequencing events

Materials: flannelboard, white pompon, fabric paint, pipe cleaner, cutouts (see list below), *The Very Hungry Caterpillar* by Eric Carle

Cutout (pattern page number):

1 leaf-shaped cutout—*Use a small white pompon for the caterpillar's egg.*
1 caterpillar (60)—*Cut out body using pinking shears. Add dabs of fabric paint for eyes and a nose.*
1 apple (61)
2 pears (61)
3 plums (61)
4 strawberries (60)—*Add dots of black fabric paint for markings.*
5 orange circles for oranges
1 brown square for a piece of cake
1 pink circle—*Glue it to a brown triangle for an ice-cream cone.*
1 pickle (61)
1 yellow rectangle—*Cut holes into it for a cheese slice.*
1 blue circle for a lollipop—*Add a white swirling line of fabric paint and glue a pipe cleaner on the back.*
1 brown triangle for a cherry pie slice
1 brown sausage (60)
1 cupcake (54)—*Add fabric-paint "sprinkles" on the cupcake.*
1 watermelon slice (56)—*Add black felt "seeds," a green felt "rind," and a line of white fabric paint.*
1 brown puffy cloud shape for a cocoon
1 butterfly (62)—*Decorate the wings with felt pieces and fabric paint.*

Cut a slit in each food cutout so the hungry caterpillar can "eat" its way through the food. Give each child a cutout. (Give the child with the leaf the white pompon "egg.") Arrange the children in front of the flannelboard so that they are in the order their cutouts appear in *The Very Hungry Caterpillar* by Eric Carle. Read the story slowly. Let the children illustrate the action by placing the appropriate cutouts on the flannelboard. Have the child holding the apple slide the caterpillar through the apple, the child with the two pears slide the caterpillar through both pears, and so on. The children will love illustrating this story on the flannelboard again and again. Making all the cutouts is well worth the effort!

Read About Sequencing

Look Out, Bird! Marilyn Janovitz (North-South Books, 1994)

Teddy Bear, Teddy Bear, Michael Hague (Morrow Junior, 1993)

The Very Hungry Caterpillar, Eric Carle (Philomel, 1969)

Classifying

Help young children learn to identify things that go together and to group or sort objects by different attributes using these activities.

Two Legs, Four Legs

Classifying animals

Materials: flannelboard, magazine or calendar photos of two-legged and four-legged animals, two 12-inch-diameter circles of fabric, Velcro ("hooks" strip)

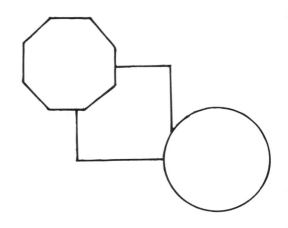

Mount each photo on a construction-paper frame. Attach a "hooks" piece of Velcro to the back of each photo. Randomly place some animals on the flannelboard. Put the circles underneath the animals. Point to each animal and ask this question: *How many legs does this animal have?* Then tell the children to help you group the animals into two groups. Designate one circle for the two-legged animals and the other circle for the four-legged animals. Then let the children take turns placing the animals on the appropriate circles. Try this again using different animal cutouts.

People and Animals

Classifying animals and people

Materials: flannelboard, variety of animal cutouts (pattern pages 62–63), varying sizes of boy and girl cutouts (pattern page 59), strip of fabric

Place the strip vertically in the middle of the flannelboard. Spread out the cutouts on the floor. Let the children take turns sorting the animal and child cutouts into two groups on the flannelboard.

Shape Up!

Classifying shapes

Materials: flannelboard, several each of six different geometric cutouts (pattern pages 52–53)

Choose three different geometric shapes. Put one of each shape in a row at the top of the flannelboard. Spread out the rest of the shapes on the floor. Let the children take turns placing the shapes in the appropriate rows, making three columns. Try the activity again using three new geometric shapes.

Things That Are ___, Things That Are Not ____

Classifying by one attribute

Materials: flannelboard, variety of cutouts (see patterns in back of this book)

Place some cutouts on the flannelboard. Choose an attribute (such as food). Let the children help you sort the items into two groups—*Things That Are Food* and *Things That Are Not Food.*

Place new cutouts on the board and choose a new category. Let the children help you sort the cutouts using the same wording: *Things That Are ___* and *Things That Are Not ___ .*

Land or Water?

Classifying by environment

Materials: flannelboard, pieces of three colors of fabric (blue, brown, green), variety of land and water animal cutouts (pattern pages 58, 60, 62–63)

From the different fabrics make a lake cutout and a tree cutout. Put these at the top of the flannelboard to form two columns. Spread out the animal cutouts on the floor. Let the children take turns categorizing the animals by their environment—land or water.

Buttons, Buttons, Buttons

Classifying by attributes

Materials: flannelboard, variety of buttons, self-sticking Velcro ("hooks" strip)

Attach a "hooks" piece of Velcro tape to the back of each button. Randomly place some of the buttons on the flannelboard. Talk with the children about how the buttons are alike and different in size, shape, color, and number of holes. Ask questions like the following: *Which buttons have two holes? Which buttons have four holes?* Place the rest of the buttons on the flannelboard and decide on appropriate categories, such as *Buttons That Have Two Holes* and *Buttons That Don't Have Two Holes.* Let the children take turns sorting the buttons according to the categories.

Healthy Choices
Sorting food items

Materials: flannelboard, variety of food cutouts (pattern pages 54, 56, 60–61), stick of wrapped gum, variety of lightweight wrapped candy, self-sticking Velcro ("hooks" strip)

Attach a "hooks" piece of Velcro to each piece of candy and to the gum wrapper. Place the candy and the food cutouts on the flannelboard. Talk with the children about examples of healthy snacks and sugary snacks. Let the children help you sort the items into two groups: *Healthy Snacks* and *Sugary Snacks.* As a follow-up activity, offer the children a healthy snack, such as pretzels or cheese and crackers, on which to munch!

How Does It Feel?
Sorting by texture

Materials: flannelboard, fabric squares in a variety of textures (fur, burlap, netting, sandpaper, aluminum foil, cardboard, etc.), self-sticking Velcro ("hooks" strip)

Attach a "hooks" piece of Velcro to the back of each square. Give each child a square. Tell the children to carefully touch their squares and ask them the following questions: *Is your square soft? Is it hard? Is it rough? Is it smooth? Is it bumpy?* Help the children sort their squares on the flannelboard by texture.

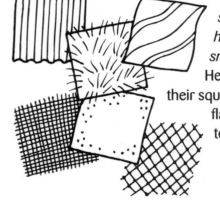

Sorting Shapes
Sorting by attributes

Materials: flannelboard, geometric cutouts (three of each) in varying sizes (make some shapes the same color and some different colors; pattern pages 52–53)

Randomly put six of the cutouts on the flannelboard. Ask the children, *How are these shapes alike?* Help the children see similarities in shape, size, color, number of sides, or number of corners. Decide on an attribute by which to sort the shapes (such as *Shapes That Have Four Corners*

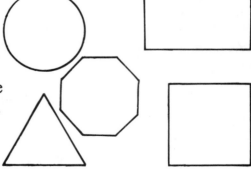

and *Shapes That Don't Have Four Corners*). Arrange the shapes into the two groups on the flannelboard. Then ask the children, *Is there another way to group these shapes?* Help the children find another way to group the shapes (such as *Shapes That Are the Same Size* and *Shapes That Aren't the Same Size).* Rearrange the shapes into two new groups. Try this activity again using a different set of shapes.

Slow or Fast

Sorting by speed

Materials: flannelboard, variety of animal cutouts (pattern pages 55, 58, 60, 62–63)

Spread the animal cutouts on the floor. Randomly place six of the animals on the flannelboard. Talk with the children about how some animals move fast and some move slowly. Let a child sort the animals on the flannelboard into two groups—*Fast Animals* and *Slow Animals*. Place six different animals on the flannelboard and let the children sort them by speed.

Alike and Different Animals

Alike and different

Materials: flannelboard, variety of animal cutouts (pattern pages 55, 58, 60, 62–63), six-inch-diameter fabric circle

Place the circle in the middle of the flannelboard. Randomly put four animals outside of the circle. Ask the children, *How are these alike?* Help the children see any similarities in size, color, or other attribute. Decide on a common attribute (such as *Animals That Are Pets*). Place animals on the circle. Then ask the children, *How are these animals different?* Help the children find something different about the animals, such as color or the way they move. Remove those animals from the circle.

How Animals Move

Sorting by attributes, multiple attributes

Materials: flannelboard, variety of animal cutouts (pattern pages 55, 58, 60, 62–63), three strips of fabric, mini-sentence strips, two 6-inch-diameter fabric circles, Velcro ("hooks" strip)

Write the words *crawl, hop, fly, swim,* and *walk* on separate sentence strips. Attach a "hooks" piece of Velcro to the back of each strip. Arrange the circles on the flannelboard so that they somewhat overlap. Spread out the animals on the floor. Talk with the children about the different ways animals move. As you introduce each movement word, put it on the flannelboard and have a child demonstrate the movement. Place one category (sentence strip) above each circle on the flannelboard. Say to the children: *Find animals that can (movement word) and place it on this circle. Find animals that can (different movement word) and place it on this circle.* Let the children take turns sorting the animals into the two groups. If an animal belongs in both categories, say to the children: *We will place the animal where the two circles overlap to show that this animal can move both ways.* Then choose two different categories, and let the children sort the animals again.

Read About Classifying

Biggest, Strongest, Fastest, Steve Jenkins (Scholastic, 1995)

The Button Box, Margarette S. Reid (Dutton, 1990)

Is It Rough? Is It Smooth? Is It Shiny? Tana Hoban (Greenwillow, 1984)

Moving Day, Robert Kalan (Greenwillow, 1996)

Red Day, Green Day, Edith Kunhardt (Greenwillow, 1992)

One-to-One Correspondence

These flannelboard activities give young children practice in pairing or matching people, animals, and things.

Hanging Up the Laundry

One-to-one correspondence

Materials: flannelboard, T-shirt shapes cut from a variety of fabrics, small basket, clothespins (one for each T-shirt), self-sticking Velcro ("hooks" strip)

Attach a "hooks" piece of Velcro to the back of each clothespin. Place all the T-shirts in the basket. Let the children take turns "hanging up" a T-shirt on each clothespin!

Matching Mittens

One-to-one correspondence

Materials: flannelboard, pairs of mitten shapes cut from a variety of fabrics, small basket

Place all the mittens in the basket. Let the children take turns pairing up the mittens and placing the pairs on the flannelboard for all to see.

Cars and Garages

One-to-one correspondence

Materials: flannelboard, car cutouts (in six different colors) and car wheel cutouts (pattern page 57), six different colors of fabric that match the cars

Attach two black wheel cutouts to each car by using brass fasteners. Cut a rectangular "garage" and a triangular "roof" out of each color of fabric. Spread the cutouts on the floor. Let the children take turns matching a roof to each garage and placing both pieces on the flannelboard. Then let the children pair up a car with each garage.

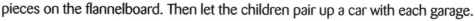

Animal Babies

One-to-one correspondence

Materials: flannelboard, variety of animal cutouts (one big and one little of each animal; pattern pages 58, 62–63)

Give each child a little animal cutout. Spread out the big animal cutouts on the floor. Tell the children that the big animals are the "mommies and daddies" of the baby animals they are holding. Let each child pair up his or her baby animal with its parent and place both pieces on the flannelboard. Then mix up all the animals. Let the children take turns matching parents and babies.

Walking Pets

One-to-one correspondence

Materials: flannelboard, variety of animal cutouts (pattern pages 58, 62–63), varying sizes of child cutouts (pattern page 59)

Randomly place the child cutouts on the flannelboard. Spread the animal cutouts on the floor. Let the children take turns matching one pet to one child.

Animal Homes

One-to-one correspondence

Materials: flannelboard, one each of the rabbit, bird, snake, and fish cutouts (pattern pages 58, 62–63); brown, blue, and green pieces of fabric; fabric paint; wiggly eyes

Add fabric-paint mouths, noses, and whiskers on the animals. Glue on wiggly eyes or add dabs of fabric paint for eyes. Cut an oval-shaped "snake hole" out of the brown fabric. Cut the shape of a hill out of the green fabric for the rabbit's home. Cut the shape of a pond out of the blue fabric for the fish's home. Cut two-inch-long strips from the brown fabric and arrange them into a bird's nest.

Place the four animal homes on the flannelboard. Talk with the children about how their own homes look, and talk about each of the animal homes. Then give each animal cutout to a child. Have those children take turns matching the animals with their homes. Repeat this again using different children.

Listening

Develop better listening skills in young children with these flannelboard activities.

Cat in the Hat

Listening, positional words

Materials: flannelboard, top hat–shaped cutout, cat cutout (pattern page 63), fabric paint, yarn

Add fabric-paint eyes, nose, mouth, and whiskers on the cat. Attach a yarn tail.

Place the top hat on the flannelboard. Tell the children to listen carefully as you tell where to place the cat. Then say something like the following: *The cat is beside the hat.* Let children take turns moving the cat to different positions.

Left, Right, Middle, Top, and Bottom

Listening

Materials: flannelboard, five different cutouts (see variety of patterns in back of this book)

Spread the cutouts on the floor. Let the children take turns placing each cutout on the flannelboard in a specific place— *left, right, middle, top,* or *bottom.* Direct each child by saying something like the following: *Place the car on the left.*

Jump, Frog, Jump!

Listening, sequencing, color recognition

Materials: flannelboard, three 3" x 4" strips cut from three different solid colors of fabric, frog cutout (pattern page 63)

Place the three strips in a row on the flannelboard. Tell the children these are three logs. Hold up the frog cutout and tell the children to listen carefully as you tell which log the frog jumped on first, second, and third. Say to the children: *Frog jumped*

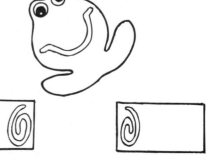

*on the **(color)** log first. Next, he jumped on the **(color)** log. Then he jumped on the **(color)** log.* Ask for a volunteer to show how the frog jumped. Each time the child moves the frog to a log, have the children say *jump, frog, jump!*

Napping on the Bed

Listening, sequencing

Materials: flannelboard, six animal cutouts (pattern pages 62–63), boy and girl cutouts (pattern page 59), bed-shaped cutout, *The Napping House* by Audrey Wood (Harcourt Brace, 1984)

Add details to the bed by attaching a cotton-ball pillow. Add facial details to the animals and children using fabric paint.

Read aloud *The Napping House.* Place the bed cutout on the flannelboard. Spread the other cutouts on the floor. Say to the children something like the following: *In our napping house a boy is sleeping on the bed. A cat is sleeping next to the boy. And the mouse is sleeping next to the cat.* Invite children to place the cutouts in order on the bed. Do this again and again. Challenge the children by using more cutouts each time!

Where's the Bug?

Listening, ordinal numbers

Materials: flannelboard, six leaf cutouts and one bug cutout (pattern page 55), fabric paint, wiggly eyes

Use fabric paint and wiggly eyes to add details to the bug.

Place the leaves in a row on the flannelboard. Have the children close their eyes while you hide the bug under one of the leaves. Say to the children while their eyes are still closed: *The bug is hiding under the (ordinal number) leaf.* Have the children open their eyes and ask for a volunteer to find the bug. This is such fun that the children will want to do it again and again!

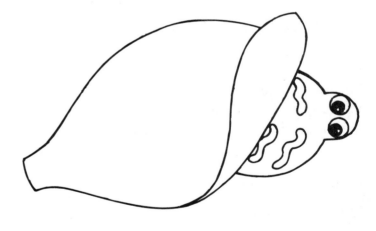

Visual Memory

Use these activities to help young children develop their ability to remember what is seen and to identify things missing from what was seen.

Apples on an Apple Tree

Visual memory, counting

Materials: flannelboard, 20 red fabric circles, large "tree" made from green and brown fabrics

Place the tree pieces on the flannelboard. Put 10 red "apples" on the tree. Have the children close their eyes while you remove some of the apples. Have the children tell you how many apples are missing. Challenge the children by putting more than 10 apples on the tree.

Items in a Row

Ordering

Materials: flannelboard, variety of cutouts (see patterns in the back of this book)

Arrange four cutouts in a certain order on the flannelboard. Have the children close their eyes while you change the order of the cutouts. Invite a child to put the cutouts back in the original order. Repeat this several times. Challenge the children by ordering more than four cutouts!

What's Missing?

Visual memory

Materials: flannelboard, variety of geometric cutouts to form a robot (pattern pages 52–53), buttons, pompons, pipe cleaners, self-sticking Velcro ("hooks" strip)

Arrange the cutouts to form a robot on the flannelboard. Attach a "hooks" piece of Velcro to each button. Place the buttons on the robot. Cut the pipe cleaners to make the robot's antennae. Use the pompons for eyes.

Introduce the robot to the children! Then have the children close their eyes while you remove an item from the robot. Have the children tell you what's missing.

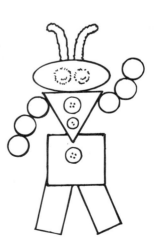

What's Different?

Visual memory

Materials: flannelboard, variety of cutouts (see patterns in back of this book)

Arrange the cutouts to create a picture on the flannelboard. Have the children close their eyes while you change something in the picture. Have the children tell you what's different in the picture.

Food in the Fridge

Visual memory

Materials: flannelboard, variety of food cutouts (see pattern pages 54, 56, 60–61), large fabric rectangle

Place four of the food cutouts on the flannelboard. Tell the children you are putting the food in the refrigerator, and cover the cutouts with the rectangle. Have the children tell you the names of the food in the refrigerator. Repeat this several times using different foods each time.

Caterpillar Eggs

Visual memory

Materials: flannelboard, two leaf cutouts (pattern page 55), small white pompons

Place the leaf cutouts on the flannelboard. Put different amounts of pompon "caterpillar eggs" on each leaf. Have the children close their eyes, and ask them questions such as the following: *How many eggs are on the first leaf? How many eggs are on the second leaf?* Repeat the activity, changing the number of eggs on each leaf.

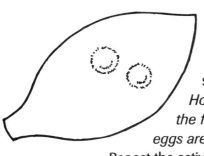

Look Out for Shapes

Visual memory

Materials: flannelboard, variety of geometric cutouts (make some the same color; pattern pages 52–53)

Place some of the cutouts on the flannelboard. Have the children close their eyes, and ask them questions such as the following: *How many red shapes are on the flannelboard? How many green shapes? How many circles are on the flannelboard?* Repeat the activity with different shapes.

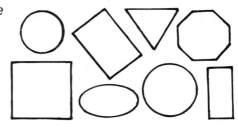

J330003 Using Flannelboards to Teach Basic Skills

Vocabulary Development

Help young children identify new words and learn their meanings with these flannelboard activities.

Bug on a Rug

Vocabulary development, positional words

Materials: flannelboard, bug cutout (pattern page 55), oval-shaped piece of fabric for a "rug"

Let the children take turns positioning the bug cutout in relation to the rug. Give the children different instructions using positional words. (For example: *Put the bug on the rug. Put the bug under the rug.*)

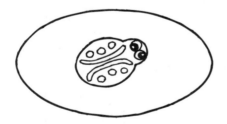

The Grocery Store

Vocabulary development, oral language

Materials: flannelboard, variety of food cutouts (pattern pages 54, 56, 60-61; see descriptions on how to decorate food on page 35), small basket

Place the food on the flannelboard. Invite children one at a time to "shop" for food as the rest of the children chant this rhyme:

*(name of child) went shopping
At the grocery store,
(name of child) bought a(n) (food cutout),
Then walked out the door!*

Have the shopper put the food cutout in the basket and hand the basket to another child. Repeat the activity until the store is empty!

What's Behind My Back?

Vocabulary development, oral language

Materials: flannelboard, variety of cutouts (see patterns in back of this book)

Place all the cutouts on the flannelboard. Have the children close their eyes, and invite a child to choose a cutout and hold it behind his or her back. Tell the children to open their eyes. Have the child holding the cutout describe it without saying its name. Let the rest of the children try to guess the name of the cutout!

Making Flowers Grow

Vocabulary development, oral language

Materials: flannelboard; flower, leaf, and seed cutouts (pattern page 55); one 3-inch-long strip of green fabric; raindrop and sun cutouts (pattern page 64); four 1-inch lengths of white yarn; strip of light brown fabric the length of the flannelboard; mini-sentence strips; Velcro ("hooks" strip)

Write the words *soil, seed, water, sun, roots, stem, leaf,* and *flower* on separate sentence strips. Attach a "hooks" piece of Velcro to the back of each strip. Place the brown fabric along the bottom of the flannelboard to represent the soil. Spread the cutouts on the floor. Then follow this script:

Let's grow a flower. First we need good soil.
(Place the *soil* label on the brown fabric.)

Then we plant a seed in the soil.
(Let a child place the seed on the soil. Put the *seed* label next to the seed.)

Next we water the seed and let it grow in the sunshine.
(Have children place the sun and the raindrop on the flannelboard. Arrange labels.)

Let's watch our flower grow. First the roots grow down into the soil.
(Place the yarn "roots" under the seed. Put the *roots* label next to the roots.)

Then the stem grows.
(Arrange the stem [strip of green fabric] and its label.)

Next the leaves grow.
(Put the leaf on the stem and arrange its label.)

Finally a flower grows!
(Arrange the flower and its label.)

Then teach the children this "Flower Song" (sung to the tune of "Twinkle, Twinkle Little Star"):

> *What makes flowers*
> *Grow so tall,*
> *From a seed*
> *That is so small?*
>
> *Sun and water,*
> *Soil makes three—*
> *Mother Nature's mystery!*
>
> *Here's the flower*
> *Standing tall,*
> *I cannot see*
> *The seed at all!*

Day and Night

Use these flannelboard activities to introduce young children to the concept of shadows and to give them practice in classifying daytime and nighttime events.

Guessing Game

Verbal expression, classifying night and day

Materials: flannelboard, sun cutout (pattern page 64), crescent moon–shaped cutout

Talk with the children about the activities they do during the daytime and the activities they do at nighttime. Then invite a child to describe an activity that he or she does (such as eat breakfast) without telling the activity's name or when it's done. Let the rest of the children guess if it's a daytime or nighttime activity. To make a guess, a child places the sun or the moon on the flannelboard. Whoever guesses correctly gets to describe the next activity.

Animal Days and Nights

Classifying animals, oral language

For each pair of animals use fabric paint to make one face awake and one face sleeping. Place the sun on the left side of the flannelboard and the moon on the right side. Let the children take turns placing each animal under the appropriate symbol for day or for night.

Materials: flannelboard, lap-sized flannelboards (one for each pair of children), two each of several animal cutouts (use animals that sleep at night; see variety of patterns in back of this book), sun cutout (pattern page 64), crescent moon–shaped cutout, fabric paint

For an extension activity, place the children into groups of two, and give each group two animals and a lap-sized flannelboard. Let the children spend time making up stories about what their animals did during the day and what they did at night. Invite the children to share their stories on the big flannelboard.

Matching Shadows

One-to-one correspondence, visual discrimination

Materials: flannelboard, two each of a variety of animal cutouts (cut one from gray fabric and cut the other from a color fabric; see patterns in back of this book), flashlight

Tell the children that in the daytime the sun shines on them and around them. It doesn't shine through them. Their bodies block the light and make shadows.

Shine a flashlight on the wall and demonstrate how to make shadows with your hands. Let the children take turns making hand shadows. Then spread out the color animal cutouts and their gray "shadows." Let each child match an animal with its shadow on the flannelboard. As a follow-up activity, take the children outside, if it's a sunny day, and let them make shadows with their bodies!

Daytime, Nighttime

Classifying pictures of day and night activities

Materials: flannelboard, crescent moon–shaped cutout, sun cutout (pattern page 64), simple pictures showing daytime and nighttime activities (use old workbooks, coloring books, and calendars), construction paper, self-sticking Velcro ("hooks" strip)

Mount each picture on a piece of construction paper to make a sturdy backing and frame. Attach a "hooks" piece of Velcro to the back of each frame. Place the sun on the left side of the flannelboard and the moon on the right side. Hold up a picture of an activity. Ask the children, *Do you think this is a daytime activity or a nighttime activity?* Let the children take turns placing each cutout under the appropriate symbol: sun for day or moon for night.

Read About Light and Shadows

Bear Shadow, Frank Asch (Putnam, 1985)

Goodnight Moon, Margaret Wise Brown (Harper & Row, 1947)

Light, Donald Crews (Greenwillow, 1981)

What Makes a Shadow? Clyde Robert Bulla (HarperCollins, 1962)

Weather and the Seasons

Use these activities to introduce young children to the concept of weather and the sequence of the seasons—fall, winter, spring, and summer.

Favorite Weather

Graphing

Place the weather cutouts in a column on the left side of the flannelboard. Give each child one shape cutout. Ask the children the following question: *Which is your favorite kind of weather—snowy days; rainy days; hot, sunny days; windy days; or cloudy days?* Record the responses by making a graph. Let the children take turns placing their cutouts next to the corresponding symbol of their favorite weather. Then ask questions about the graph such as the following: *Which weather is the most favorite? Which weather is the least favorite? Do more children enjoy hot, sunny days or snowy days?*

Materials: flannelboard; snowflake, wind, sun, and raindrop cutouts (pattern page 64); cloud-shaped fabric cutout; several of one geometric shape (one for each child; pattern pages 52–53)

What to Wear?

Classifying, making a graph

Materials: flannelboard; snowflake, wind, sun, and raindrop cutouts (pattern page 64); cloud-shaped fabric cutout; several of one geometric shape (pattern pages 52–53); various seasonal items such as sunglasses, swim goggles, mittens, snow boots, raincoat, cap, wool hat, sandals, ice skates, and earmuffs

Place the weather cutouts in a column on the left side of the flannelboard. Make a pile of the shape cutouts. Give out each seasonal item to a child and ask him or her the following question: *When would you wear the (seasonal item)—on a snowy day, a rainy day, a sunny day, a windy day, or a cloudy day?* Make a graph by having each child place a shape cutout next to the corresponding weather symbol. When the graph is finished, ask questions such as the following: *Which kind of weather has the most items? Are more items for windy days or sunny days?* You may want to repeat this activity and give the items to different children. Since some items can be worn in different types of weather, the responses may be different.

Which Season Am I?

Dramatic skills, creative expression

Materials: flannelboard; snowflake, wind, sun, and raindrop cutouts (pattern page 64); cloud-shaped fabric cutout

Talk about the kinds of activities children might do during the different seasons. Invite individuals to pantomime activities such as skating, swimming, walking in the rain, or raking leaves that are often associated with a particular season. Let the rest of the children try to guess the season by placing the corresponding symbol on the flannelboard—wind for fall, snowflake for winter, rain for spring, and sun for summer.

Sorting Seasons

Classifying seasonal pictures

Materials: flannelboard; snowflake, wind, sun, and raindrop cutouts (pattern page 64); cloud-shaped fabric cutout; four envelopes; seasonal pictures—umbrella, sun, rain, snowman, ice skates, sunglasses, leaves—cut from magazines and old workbooks, Velcro ("hooks" strip)

Attach a "hooks" piece of Velcro to the back of each envelope. Print the name of a season on each envelope. Arrange the envelopes and their appropriate symbols in sequence on the flannelboard. Spread out the seasonal pictures on the floor. Let the children take turns matching the pictures with the seasons by placing them inside the corresponding envelopes.

Sequence the Seasons

Oral language, sequencing

Materials: flannelboard; snowflake, wind, sun, and raindrop cutouts (pattern page 64)

Put the cutouts on the flannelboard. Help the children learn to sequence the seasons by teaching them this song (sung to the tune of "Twinkle, Twinkle Little Star"):

*Winter, spring, and
Summer, fall,
Count the seasons,
Four in all!*

*Naming seasons,
Is such fun!
Say all four, and
Then you're done!*

*Winter, spring, and
Summer, fall,
Which one is
The best of all?*

Using the weather symbols to represent the seasons (wind for fall, snowflake for winter, rain for spring, and sun for summer), let a child sequence the seasons on the flannelboard while the rest of the children sing the song. Mix up the cutouts and repeat the activity with different children.

Read About Weather and Seasons

It Looked Like Spilt Milk, Charles G. Shaw (Harper & Row, 1947)

Winter Lullaby, Barbara Seuling (Harcourt Brace, 1998)

Who Is Tapping at My Window? A. G. Deming (Dutton, 1988)

rectangle

(Use with activities on pages 12–13, 16, 18, 26, 34, 36, 38, 44–45, 50.)

square

(Use with activities on pages 12–13, 15, 18, 26–27, 34, 36, 38, 44–45, 50.)

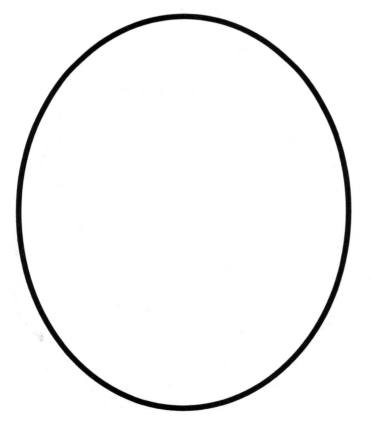

oval

(Use with activities on pages 12–13, 16, 18, 26–27, 36, 38, 44–45, 50.)

Teacher: Enlarge or reduce copies of the patterns to vary the sizes of the cutouts. Laminate or cover them with clear self-sticking paper for sturdiness. Use them as cutouts or as templates for tracing on felt or other fabrics.

J330003 Using Flannelboards to Teach Basic Skills

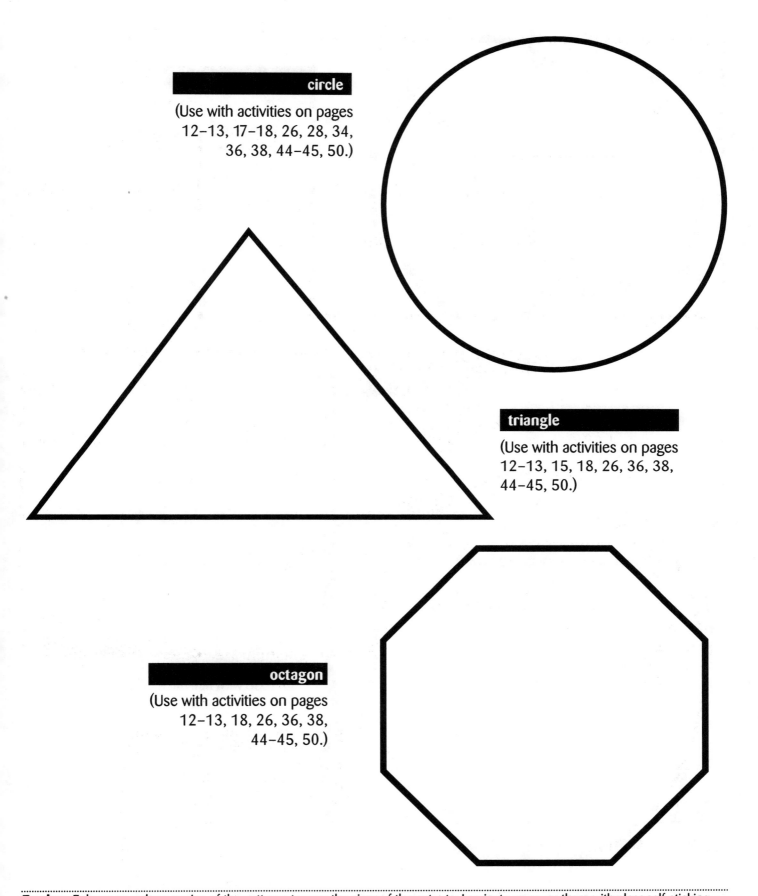

circle
(Use with activities on pages
12–13, 17–18, 26, 28, 34,
36, 38, 44–45, 50.)

triangle
(Use with activities on pages
12–13, 15, 18, 26, 36, 38,
44–45, 50.)

octagon
(Use with activities on pages
12–13, 18, 26, 36, 38,
44–45, 50.)

Teacher: Enlarge or reduce copies of the patterns to vary the sizes of the cutouts. Laminate or cover them with clear self-sticking paper for sturdiness. Use them as cutouts or as templates for tracing on felt or other fabrics.

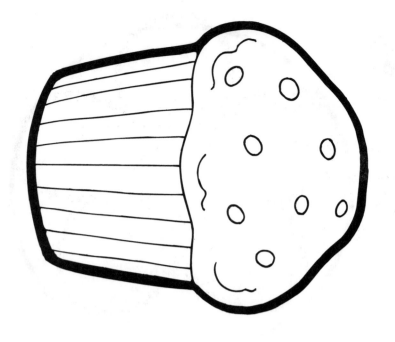

cupcake
(Use with activities on pages 20, 24, 35, 38, 45–46.)

candle
(Use with activities on pages 20, 24.)

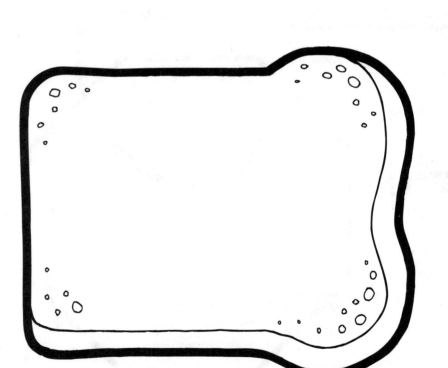

bread
(Use with activities on pages 34, 38, 45, 46.)

Teacher: Enlarge or reduce copies of the patterns to vary the sizes of the cutouts. Laminate or cover them with clear self-sticking paper for sturdiness. Use them as cutouts or as templates for tracing on felt or other fabrics.

flower

(Use with activities on pages
11, 14, 22, 47.)

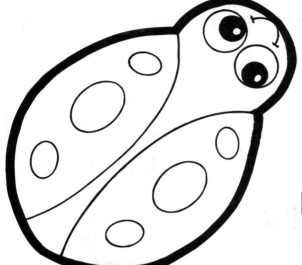

bug

(Use with activities on pages
11, 18, 31–32, 39, 43, 46.)

seed

(Use with activities on pages
11, 47.)

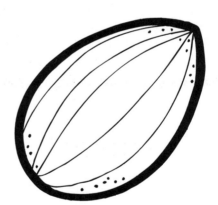

leaf

(Use with activities on pages
11, 16, 43, 45, 47.)

Teacher: Enlarge or reduce copies of the patterns to vary the sizes of the cutouts. Laminate or cover them with clear self-sticking paper for sturdiness. Use them as cutouts or as templates for tracing on felt or other fabrics.

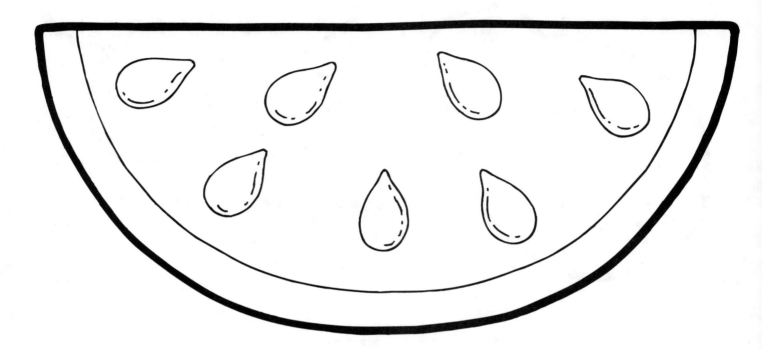

watermelon

(Use with activities on pages
15, 23, 35, 38, 45, 46.)

watermelon seeds

(Use with activities on pages
15, 23, 35, 38, 45, 46.)

Teacher: Enlarge or reduce copies of the patterns to vary the sizes of the cutouts. Laminate or cover them with clear self-sticking paper for sturdiness. Use them as cutouts or as templates for tracing on felt or other fabrics.

(Use with activities on pages 19, 40.)

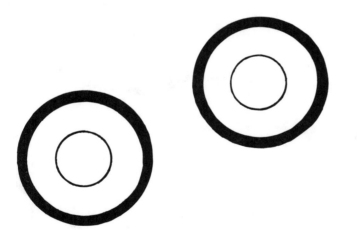

(Use with activities on pages 19, 40.)

Teacher: Enlarge or reduce copies of the patterns to vary the sizes of the cutouts. Laminate or cover them with clear self-sticking paper for sturdiness. Use them as cutouts or as templates for tracing on felt or other fabrics.

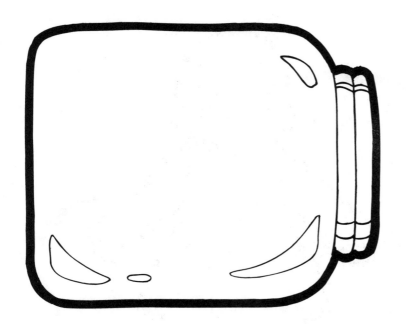

jar

(Use with activities on pages 16–17.)

mouse

(Use with activities on pages 17, 19–20, 27, 31–33, 37, 39, 41.)

snake

(Use with activities on pages 17, 31–33, 37, 39, 41.)

Teacher: Enlarge or reduce copies of the patterns to vary the sizes of the cutouts. Laminate or cover them with clear self-sticking paper for sturdiness. Use them as cutouts or as templates for tracing on felt or other fabrics.

boy

(Use with activities on pages
28, 36, 41, 43.)

Teacher: Enlarge or reduce copies of the patterns to vary the sizes of the cutouts. Laminate or cover them with clear self-sticking paper for sturdiness. Use them as cutouts or as templates for tracing on felt or other fabrics.

strawberry

(Use with activities on pages 33, 35, 38, 45, 46.)

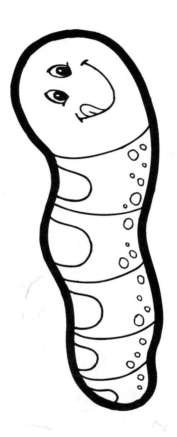

caterpillar

(Use with activities on pages 25, 31–33, 35, 37, 39.)

sausage

(Use with activities on pages 33, 35, 38, 45–46.)

Teacher: Enlarge or reduce copies of the patterns to vary the sizes of the cutouts. Laminate or cover them with clear self-sticking paper for sturdiness. Use them as cutouts or as templates for tracing on felt or other fabrics.

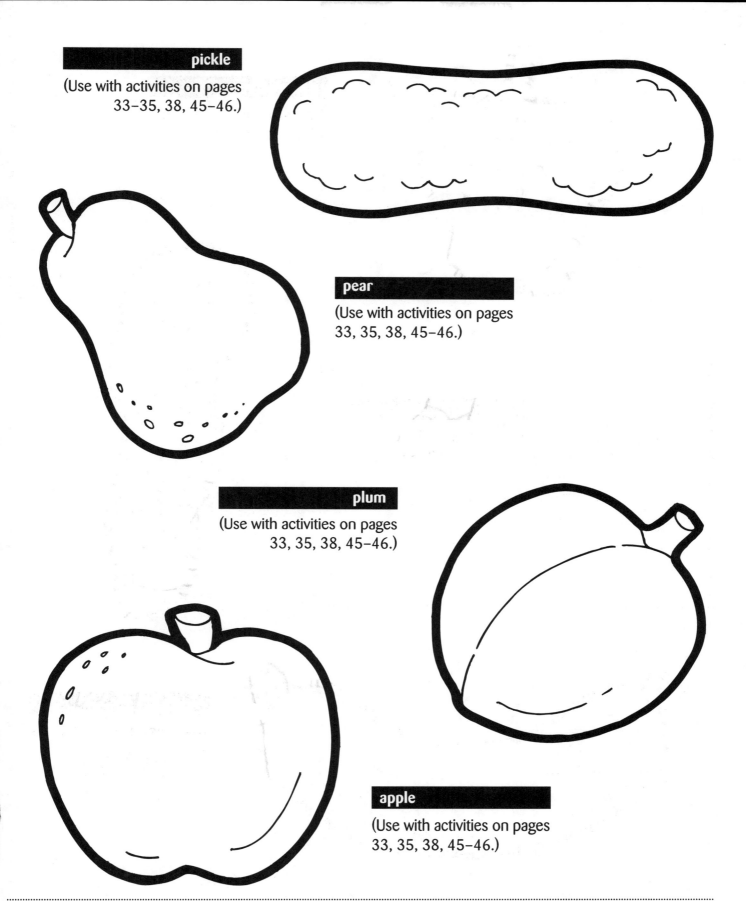

pickle
(Use with activities on pages 33–35, 38, 45–46.)

pear
(Use with activities on pages 33, 35, 38, 45–46.)

plum
(Use with activities on pages 33, 35, 38, 45–46.)

apple
(Use with activities on pages 33, 35, 38, 45–46.)

Teacher: Enlarge or reduce copies of the patterns to vary the sizes of the cutouts. Laminate or cover them with clear self-sticking paper for sturdiness. Use them as cutouts or as templates for tracing on felt or other fabrics.

Teacher: Enlarge or reduce copies of the patterns to vary the sizes of the cutouts. Laminate or cover them with clear self-sticking paper for sturdiness. Use them as cutouts or as templates for tracing on felt or other fabrics.

rabbit

(Use with activities on pages 20, 24, 30–33, 37, 39, 41, 43.)

frog

(Use with activities on pages 20, 24, 30–33, 37, 39, 41–43.)

dog

(Use with activities on pages 20, 24, 30–33, 37, 39, 41, 43.)

cat

(Use with activities on pages 20, 23–24, 30–33, 37, 39, 41–43.)

Teacher: Enlarge or reduce copies of the patterns to vary the sizes of the cutouts. Laminate or cover them with clear self-sticking paper for sturdiness. Use them as cutouts or as templates for tracing on felt or other fabrics.

(Use with activities on pages 50–51.)

snowflake

(Use with activities on pages 50–51.)

raindrop

(Use with activities on pages 47, 50–51.)

sun

(Use with activities on pages 47–51.)

Teacher: Enlarge or reduce copies of the patterns to vary the sizes of the cutouts. Laminate or cover them with clear self-sticking paper for sturdiness. Use them as cutouts or as templates for tracing on felt or other fabrics.